AF815494

Bigger than You

Bigger than You: Big Data and Obesity

An Inquiry toward Decelerationist Aesthetics

Katherine Behar

BIGGER THAN YOU: BIG DATA AND OBESITY
AN INQUIRY TOWARD DECELERATIONIST AESTHETICS
© KATHERINE BEHAR, 2016

This work carries a Creative Commons BY-NC-SA 4.0 International license, which means that you are free to copy and redistribute the material in any medium or format, and you may also remix, transform and build upon the material, as long as you clearly attribute the work to the authors (but not in a way that suggests the authors or punctum books endorses you and your work), you do not use this work for commercial gain in any form whatsoever, and that for any remixing and transformation, you distribute your rebuild under the same license. http://creativecommons.org/licenses/by-nc-sa/4.0/

First published in 2016
punctum books, Earth, Milky Way
www.punctumbooks.com

ISBN-13: 978-0692652831
ISBN-10: 0692652833

Library of Congress Cataloging Data
is available from the Library of Congress

Copy editing by Lisa Delgado.
Interior design provided by
Athabasca University Press (adapted).

For families

Contents

Acknowledgments

Versions of this essay were presented in prior contexts and this text benefits from the generous feedback received on those occasions. In 2012 I presented this project for the "Object-Oriented Feminism 2—Closer" panel at the "Nonhuman" conference convened by the Society for Literature, Science, and the Arts (SLSA). I thank copanelists Jamie "Skye" Bianco, Ian Bogost, Patricia Ticineto Clough, N. Katherine Hayles, Timothy Morton, Steven Shaviro, and Anne Pollock, respondent Eileen Joy, and the members of SLSA who contributed to our discussions.

Another presentation of this work was included in "Fat, Black Monkeys: Systems Thinking and Critical Culture in the Choreography of The Other," a panel and workshop at Stanford University's Department of Theater & Performance Studies

(TAPS) in 2013. For conceiving and hosting this event, I thank Grisha Coleman and Jennifer Brody, respectively. I am further grateful to copanelists Stephanie Leigh Batiste and Deborah Forster, and to the workshop participants in TAPS for their brilliant engagements with these ideas.

Most recently, I presented this project at a salon organized by an interdisciplinary artists' collective in Boston in 2015. I thank Nate Greenslit and all those in attendance for their tremendous comments and conversation.

Finally, my deepest gratitude goes to those who kindly agreed to read drafts of this essay and patiently talk through the ideas with me. For her exhaustive editorial eye, I thank Lisa Delgado. And for offering wise insights and kind encouragement, I thank Irina Aristarkhova, Ken Behar, Patricia Ticineto Clough, Alex Galloway, Alex Golden, Eileen Joy, Katie King, David Lukowski, Molly Mac, Anne Pollock, Trevor Smith, and Ruslan Trusewych.

Introduction

> *I shall consider human actions and appetites just as if it were a question of lines, planes, and bodies.*
>
> —Spinoza, in *Ethics*

This quote from Spinoza seems an unlikely launching pad for a discussion of the new intimacies arising between humans' bigness and big data. Yet, by considering human activities through the elegant, elemental figures of geometry, we shall see how Spinoza gets us straight into the thick thicknesses of things.

Big data refers to the massive quantity of records that are captured, amassed, and mined in the wake of digitally structured actions. It is the sum total of records of actions—the exponential archive of every component transaction captured in every data trail. These actions may originate from human or nonhuman protagonists (e.g., online shoppers or particle accelerators) and may describe human or nonhuman referents (e.g., medical data or atmospheric data). But this essay will not address data generated by or descriptive of nonhuman objects. Instead, I will adopt an object-oriented feminist perspective, arriving at the nonhuman by following big data as it restructures the human.[1] Beginning with the work that humans—in the conventional sense, individual subjects—do as the producers of big data, I'll describe how, by wielding Spinoza's "lines, planes, and bodies," big data unproduces and deindividualizes its subjects to become transhuman objects, something, I'll argue, far *vaguer* than any small subject could be.

This essay will also show how, through its materiality, big data models what I call *decelerationist aesthetics*. In decelerationist aesthetics, the aesthetic properties, proclivities, and performances of objects come to defy the accelerationist imperative to be nimbly individuated.[2] Decelerationist aesthetics rejects atomistic, liberal, humanist subjects; this unit of self is too consonant with capitalist relations and functions. Instead, decelerationist aesthetics favors transhuman sociality embodied in particulate, mattered objects; the aesthetic form of such objects resists capitalist speed and immediacy by taking back and taking up space and time. In just this way, as we shall see, big data calls into question the conventions by which humans are defined as discrete entities, and individual scales of agency are made to form central binding pillars of social existence through which bodies are drawn into relations of power and pathos.

So let us begin. En route, as we work our way up to Spinoza's "lines, planes, and bodies," we'll start by taking stock of the simplest geometrical unit: the point.

AMASSING DATA POINTS

"Data is the plastic of [the] new New Economy," announces GigaOM founder Om Malik,[3] thereby suggesting—without a shred of cynicism—that like plastic, data is malleable enough to meet every conceivable need, and its resulting pervasiveness will transform every nook and cranny of the global economy. Yet we can take data's comparison to plastic in another way, too. Consider the oft-cited University of Southern California study that calculated the world's data in 2007 at 295 exabytes, which, burned to disc, would fill a stack of CDs reaching beyond the moon. This memorably staggering quantity of CDs is an appropriate analogy, because CDs are junk plastic, a breath away from landfill. Big data is plastic in this sense too—it persists, awfully, smothering us with its uselessness.

Even so, big data maintains an unshakeable aura of worth. On the one hand, enterprise stands ready to reap it, no doubt at least in part informed by the realization that humans are at real risk of depleting organic resources in the natural world.

And indeed, the buzz around big data leaves corporations breathless with anticipation over potential profit from what appears to be an inexhaustible geyser of bits. On the other hand, big data's buzz renders individual consumers breathless for a different reason; they are flushed-faced with caution and reproach, indignant over worth stolen away.

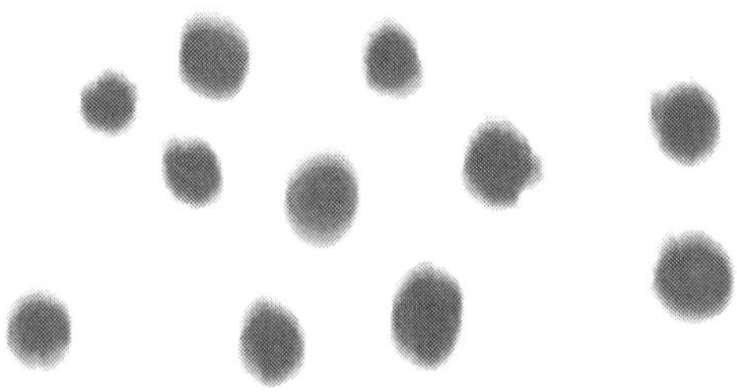

Surely enough, a major source of big data is the tracking of individuals' online activity in Internet storefronts, social media spaces, and the like. In a typical process, humans' transactions are tracked and captured in profiles in the form of personally identifiable data points, which are seamlessly aggregated by corporations, and cross compared or "mined" through analytics. Value is created when large-scale patterns, which emerge in analytics, can be tied back to the original data points and, by extension, to the profiles of individual producers and consumers.[4] Because this process occurs at multiple levels and is likely to span multiple proprietary platforms, data ownership is fraught.

As a result, many individuals take exception to what they see as the exploitation of their personal data, and protest for the establishment of legal protections[5] and technical constraints[6] to regulate the collection and use of personally identifiable data.[7] Yet, the argument to protect personal data from exploitation is an odd objection because, on the face of things, it mistakes what data under capitalism is. Is data like plastic, or is it something special, distinctive—even distinctively human?

Plainly enough, data seems to be like plastic, the product of human labor—it is, after all, produced by all that clicking. But seeing our personal data in a corporation's clutches leaves us feeling violated, and our instinctive urge to protect it amounts to treating data as no ordinary product, but something very personal: an extension, I would contend, of the physical human body. Indeed, arguments for data privacy rhetorically position data as *bodily* (deserving of the same protections from exploitation under capitalism that the body itself enjoys), rather than as a product of labor (which is fair game for capitalist exploitation).

In "The Body as Accumulation Strategy," David Harvey explains, "While capitalists may have full rights to the commodity labor power, they do not have legal rights over the person of the laborer (that would be slavery)."[8] He continues, "The capitalist has not the formal right to put the body of the person at risk . . . and working practices that do so are open to challenge."[9] I suggest that these are the same grounds on which big data practices are disputed. If we take seriously this weird recategorization of object as part-of-subject, Obama's

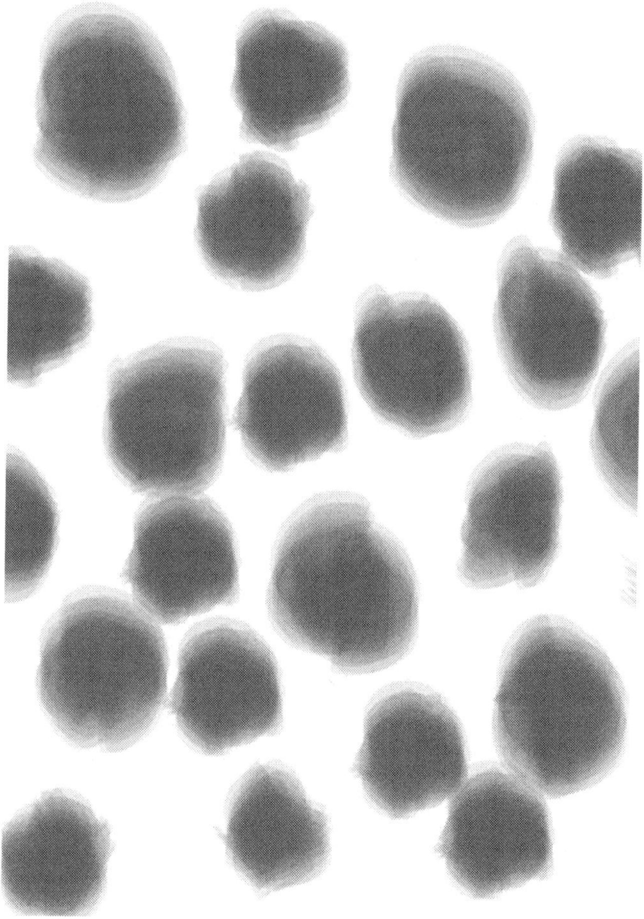

Consumer Privacy Bill of Rights[10] is directly analogous to OSHA.[11]

Note that Harvey's concerns lie with labor power, something produced by a category of action that cannot originate with any individual. Human subjects labor to make big data and have something at stake in each singular data point, but labor power happens at a "bigger" scale that is beyond the subject.

Scale, i.e., "bigness," is big data's source, its promise, and its Achilles' heel. For example, the *Economist, Forbes,* and the World Economic Forum have predicted a "data deluge,"[12] and tech journalist Colin Brown describes "a world gorging on data in the hope of turning those information streams into rivers of gold"[13]—which is to say, into a commodity just like gold, which would have minimal use value and might come to exist purely in exchange. The nightmare is to let data accumulate in unusable surpluses of unordered data points. All hopes are pinned on managing big data, efficiently processing the records that capture use to extract value for exchange. So big data is at once confusingly close to us and our bodies, and always on the verge of becoming just junk, neither useful nor exchangeable, like plastic, a hoarder's embarrassment.

Outlining data profiles

In a recent essay on big data, "'The whole is always smaller than its parts'—a digital test of Gabriel Tarde's monads," Bruno Latour et al. describe a data reduction process, a data management method for producing valuable insights by enacting delimitation in a heterogeneous field of data points. To accomplish this, Latour et al. recommend drawing a line.

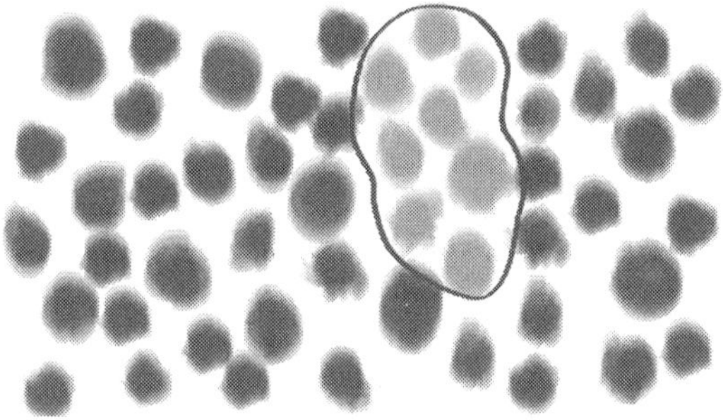

Or more specifically, they suggest drawing a potato:

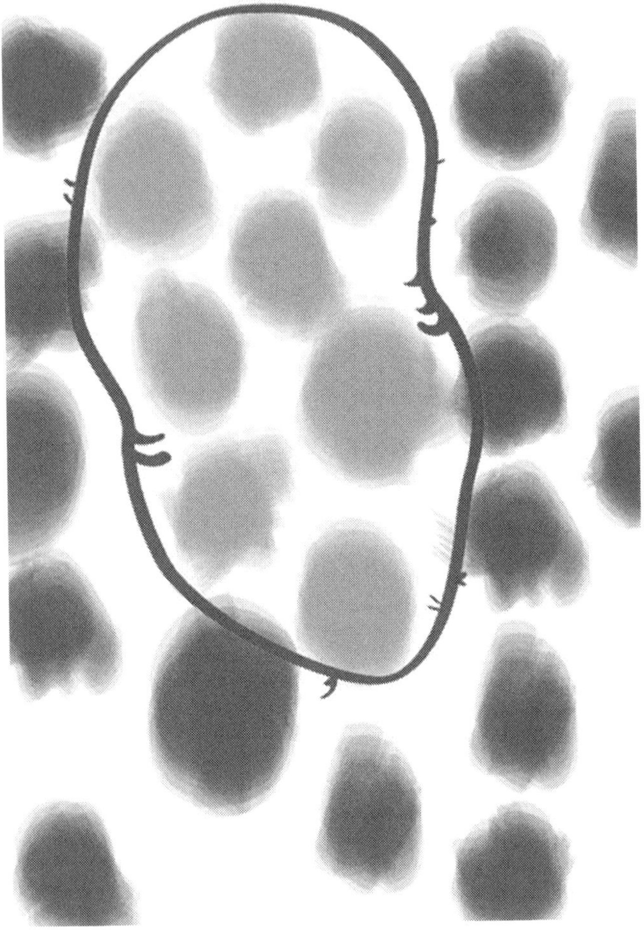

> The first [method for handling data sets] is the very humble and often unnoticed gesture we all make when we surround a list of features with a circle (a shape often referred to as a 'potato'!).[14]

Latour et al. are concerned with developing a theory that does not lapse into two levels of analysis for dealing with individuals and aggregates. Tarde's theory of monads is an elusive, "admittedly exotic notion" borrowed from Gottfried Wilhelm Leibniz. In bare terms, Latour et al. define a monad as "not a part of a whole, but a *point of view* on all other entities taken *severally* and not as a totality."[15] Tarde's monads offer the type of "one level standpoint" Latour et al. seek, and they suggest that the contemporary practice of navigating databases provides a working proof of Tarde's thought. An in-depth discussion of Tarde and Latour is beyond the scope of this essay, but it is instructive that Latour's examples are drawn from the problem of searching for the identity of a human individual within a vast data set. Latour et al. search by name—what could be more subject-oriented?—and their strategy for ordering

the undifferentiated sprawl of heterogeneous raw data is to group data points by drawing a figure. Their "humble . . . unnoticed gesture" of inscribing a line traces an edge and lends shape to a contour; they are drawing a *profile.*

A profile is a contour, a representation in outline that renders significant features. Latour's potato is precisely the use of a line to inscribe a profile into a plane of aggregated data, to create an outlined representation for the very purpose of "consider[ing] human actions and appetites." While in this particular instance Latour is, for once, after the human, his drawing operation

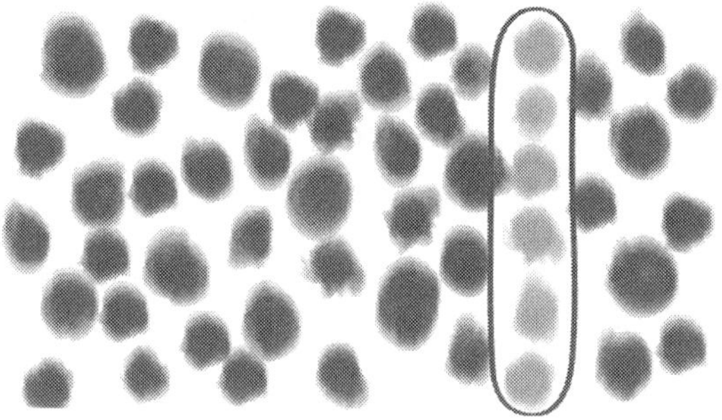

applies equally to nonhuman objects, and a similar linear gesture appears in object-oriented ontology, in the "general inscriptive strategy" Ian Bogost, following Graham Harman, calls *ontography.*[16]

According to Bogost, the most basic kind of ontography is a list, which, as you may recall, is what Latour's potato encloses. "Ontography," Bogost explains, "is an aesthetic set theory."[17]

While the potato encircles on a principle of affiliation, the list deploys a line to *line things up*, stressing difference through rhetorical disjunction.[18] Yet, both are a means of enticing a form, while allowing irreducibility.

But if the point of the profile is to render significant features, the identifiable silhouette of an individual, what are we to make of the nondescriptive graphical quality that takes place in the lining up of an ontographic list, which

according to Bogost only "reveals" "on the basis of existence" without "necessarily offering clarification or description"[19]? Rhetorical strategies aside, what good is the "profile" of this proffered potato?

Latour might demur, but he and his colleagues state, "The gesture of adding a circle is simply the recognition of the outside limit of a monad."[20] It seems that at best, this will be a lumpy approximation, too blobby for portraiture and too vague to aid identification. Surely, there comes a tipping point wherein the more detail one adds to this profile—the more points one encloses in its line—the more bloated and less descriptive it becomes. This overstuffed potato has an odd profile indeed!

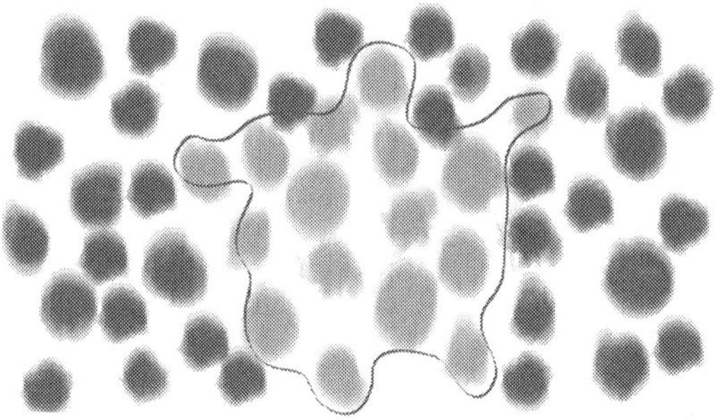

Ontography, too, is susceptible to swelling. Writes Bogost, it "is a practice of increasing the number and density. . . . Instead of removing elements to achieve the elegance of simplicity [which would be data reduction] ontography adds (or simply leaves) elements to accomplish the realism of multitude."[21] Blogger David Berry makes a suggestive link between object-oriented ontology's propensity to pack it in and Heidegger's notion of gigantism.[22] Though Berry protests the intermingling of humans and nonhumans in object-oriented litanies, the very "contamination" he fears signals the nonanthropocentric impurity this essay seeks to promote. The gigantic is a telling figure; it is a pathological figure, a figure in excess of self.

Big data's pathological overaccumulations symptomize capitalist excess, like plastic, and big data threatens to bloat a naive profile into a totality. Indeed, Latour et al. confirm, "Were the inquiry to continue, the 'whole world', as Leibniz said, would be 'grasped' or 'reflected' through this idiosyncratic point of view."[23] A thusly inflated profile recalls the David Foster Wallace character Norman Bombardini, who resolves to permanently overcome the loneliness inherent in what Tarde and Latour call a two-level-standpoint universe, divided between Self and Other, individual and aggregate.[24] Bombardini fixates on filling the entire universe with Self, squeezing Otherness out of the (profile) picture by aggressive consumption, an anti–Weight Watchers, reverse-diet plan to grow to infinite size. Like Bombardini, big data bingeing balloons a profile into another sign of big capitalist excess, another symptomatic silhouette of surplus: obesity.

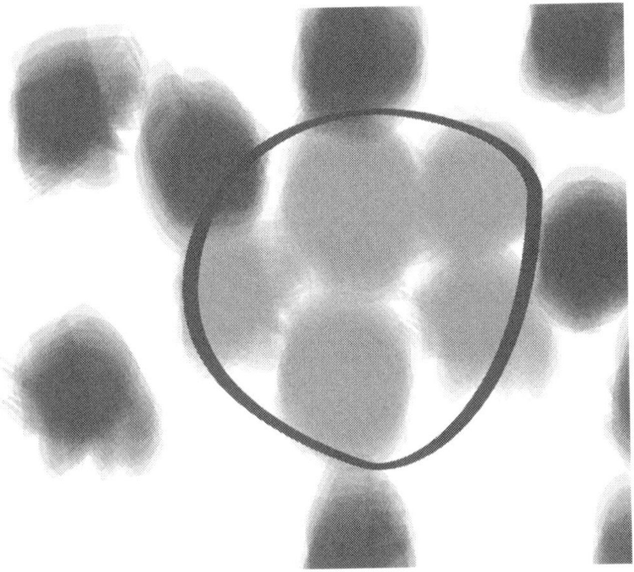

Populating a common plane

The subtitle of the essay "Slow Death" by the inimitable Lauren Berlant is a parenthetical ontograph, "(Sovereignty, Obesity, Lateral Agency)."[25] The last item, lateral agency, takes place across a common plane, zoned for occupancy[26] and populated by a host of factors and actors. Mimicking the plane's extensiveness, Berlant describes "ordinary life" as including and constituted by "spreading-out activities like sex or eating."[27] Devoting her essay to describing what is "vague and gestural about the subject"[28] (not unlike our bloated tuber), Berlant traces the slow spread of obesity's profile as "not a thing, but a cluster of factors that only looks solid at a certain distance."[29]

Bogost writes, "An ontograph is a crowd,"[30] and for Berlant, too, the cluster that coheres is collective, crowd-like. In contrast to the individual profile Latour et al. shaped by including points to reference a person, obesity precludes personhood. For Berlant, it is always "oriented toward . . . self-abeyance,"[31] toward what she calls self-suspension, as opposed to self-negation.[32] Obesity is an instance of biopower that dismantles individual sovereignty, and indeed, Berlant sees obesity's profile embodying (so to speak) biopower and its relationship to managerial control. Obesity is an endemic, not an epidemic, a chronic condition requiring perpetual management, not a crisis in need of a cure; and it deals in populations, not persons. The same could be said of big data. Both are surfeits set for management and the more we eat and click, the more management we require.

Berlant uses the term *actuarial rhetoric* to describe both the material effects of the actuarial production of data, i.e., the fat data of statistics and policy, and in a figuratively broader sense, to convey how actuarial management strives "to get the fat (the substance and the people) under control."[33] With actuarial rhetoric, obesity contains fat-as-substance, fat-as-people, and data-as-fat.

Patricia Ticineto Clough and her collaborators also deal with self-abeyance in their own strange blend of substance and people in "Notes Towards a Theory of Affect-Itself."[34] Drawing from "resonances" with information theory, the life sciences, and physics, they propose to "mov[e] beyond the laborer's body assumed in the labor theory of value [which is referred] to as the body-as-organism" to arrive at a new conception of bodies "arising out of . . . matter as informational."[35]

Echoing Berlant's individual's self-abeyance, Clough et al. cite Akseli Virtanen and Paolo Virno to describe how affective labor has been theorized as "superced[ing] the individual" through an "abstract labor-power that is in excess of any one laborer's body." Pursuing this notion further, they ask whether it is *also* "in excess of the body conceived as human organism."[36] Whereas prior theories of affective labor already started suppressing personhood in favor of populations, shedding the sanctity of the individual laborer in favor of a "social individual," Clough et al.'s radical move extends the notion of population well beyond the social individual or crowd, and into the nonhuman world, the informational world of data.

Theorizing that "the distinction between organic and non-organic matter is dissolving in relationship to information," they conclude that "labor power must be treated in terms of an abstraction [that could accommodate] bodies that are beyond the [organic/nonorganic] distinction altogether."[37] This move to view the material

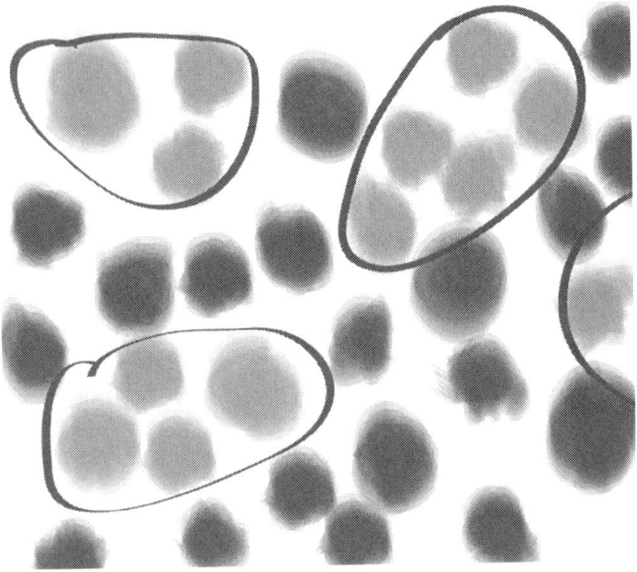

structure of labor power as informational is critical. Indeed, it is information that gives the form—fills out the profiles—of the bodies we have potatoed thus far. Recalling that for Harvey, the commodity was never data, but always the labor power traded in data's production, and that for Berlant, individual sovereignty can't be recuperated under biopower, this move to make ourselves bigger, to "spread out" into "information-as-matter," or to include data in our own mattering makes sense if we are to set our "selves" aside, self-suspending to veer toward lateral agency.

Yet, if for Clough et al. the question is whether labor power can be *in excess* of the body, I might phrase this differently: Can it *be excess body*? In other words, can labor power accrue in and as excessive bodies, obese bodies? Can labor power be fat? Clough et al. find a route into this strange transhuman matter through affect. I wonder if we can arrive at the same through bignesses, understood as both people and substance, as both big data (inorganic bodies-of-information) and big populations (obese bodies-as-organisms).

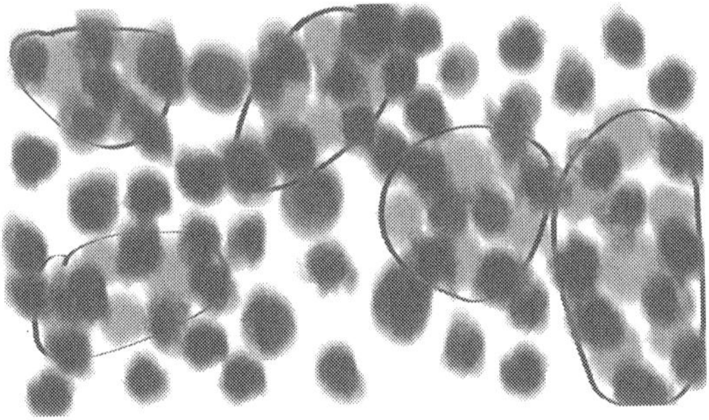

Clough's gross inclusions lend unexpected credence to the counterintuitive confusion between data as external object (product of labor) and data as included-in-subject (part of the laboring body). If affect is in matter, and an affective theory of value moves beyond the body-as-organism, we can reconsider that laboring body as including "connections between different levels of matter,"[38] including data. So the profile isn't personal. We don't produce self. We aren't who or what or how we think we are. We are, it seems, much bigger, more materially diverse, and crowd-like.

This leads us to the question of how a crowd-body that collects even-handedly such onto-graphic litanies as {self, multitude, data} or {plastic, fat, fact} or {points, lines, planes} might function. In my reading, a collective body-of-obesity/body-of-information models object-oriented feminist transhumanism and embodies decelerationist aesthetics. A transhuman body is capable of lateral agency, also described by Berlant as "the forms of spreading pleasure . . . necessary to lubricate the body's movement through capitalized time's shortened circuit."[39] If such a quite-crowded body already consists in and troubles {labor, labor power, commodity}, how else might it interface with capitalism? How might it deploy itself in relationships of power and pathos to "mov[e] through capitalized [time]"?

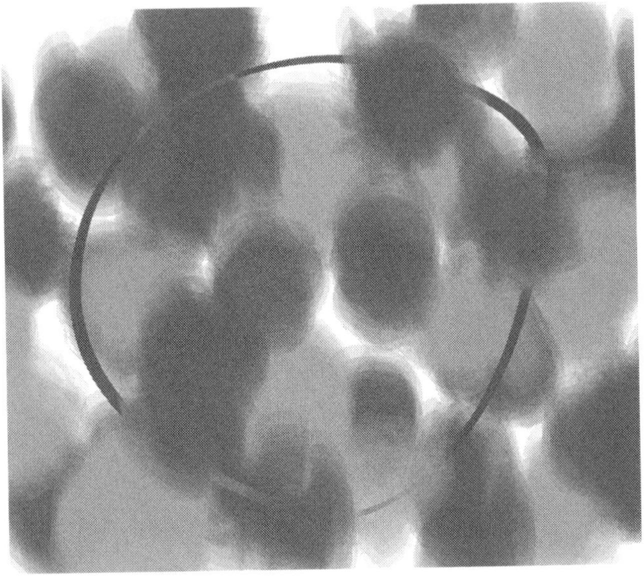

"Big" body politics

We have seen how, in the transition from point to line to plane, a body accrues information and substance and, at the same, paradoxically, becomes increasingly ill-defined. Points amass their individuality until a sense of self is lost. Lines stretch their contours until a profile is rendered indistinct. And planes sprawl until the organic and informational populations they support cross over to bear one another's resemblance. At each step we witness both accumulation (the rise of form) and ambiguity (the formlessness of form).

In an era of biopower, big data and obesity require intensive management. It is exactly this management that renders both irreparably vague. But rather than lament subjects' subsumption into something "bigger than you," I'd like to pursue, within this condition, a decelerationist form of object-oriented politics. If the tendency of "human actions and appetites" as "lines, planes, and bodies" is toward vagueness, that vagueness only awaits turning imperceptible.

If vague, a radical object-oriented feminist politics should not be expected to take the oppositional, demand-wielding forms with which we are most familiar. Just as object-oriented philosophy demotes the philosophical subject from its place of privilege, an object-oriented politics should look beyond the political subject and the dynamics of intersubjectivity that dominate political thought. One example of a political theory that accomplishes this is Elizabeth Grosz's "politics of imperceptibility."

In a critique of postcolonial feminist and antiracist politics of recognition, Grosz argues that they (as well as many political models typically cast as progressive) rely on a Hegelian model of intersubjectivity, in which the processes of recognition, identification, and subject formation are tightly intertwined.[40] It would not, I think, be stretching Grosz's point to say such politics are too subject-oriented. Rather than favor recognition and identification, which lead to the formation of *humanist* political subjects, Grosz turns to Nietzsche, whose nihilistic conception of forces leads her to an *inhuman* politics of imperceptibility, akin to what I have been calling vagueness.

Drawing from Nietzsche, she writes, "Force needs to be understood in its full sub-human and super-

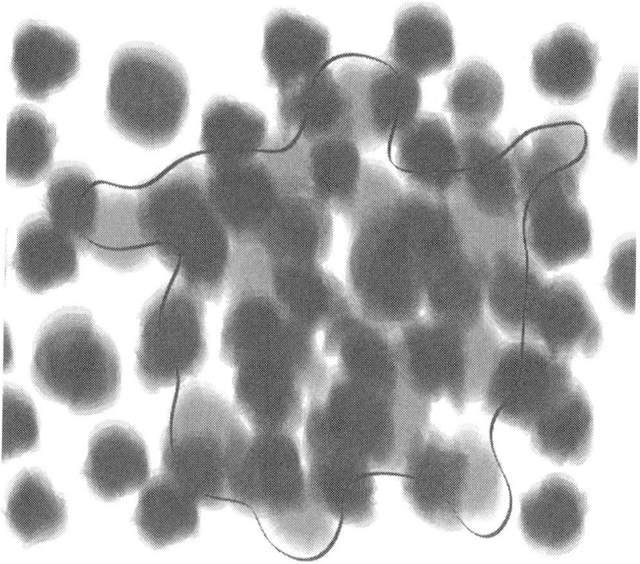

human resonances: as [Lyotard's] *inhuman* . . . which both makes the human possible and which at the same time positions the human within a world where force works in spite of and around the human."[41]

Forgoing both recognition and identification, and forsaking the subject as political agent, Grosz's inhuman politics stands in contrast to most other feminist and antiracist strategies, including Judith Butler's post-Hegelian deconstruction of the subject, which remains, for Grosz, always humanist.[42] On this important point, Grosz writes: "Denaturalizing is important. But it is not my project. We have, by now, been denaturalized as much as we need to be. What I'm much more interested in [is a] sort of renaturalizing that has been taken away, redynamizing a sort of nature."[43]

The sense that we are already thoroughly deconstructed, and that this deconstruction has only facilitated our being reprocessed and rationalized, echoes the progressive complaint against neoliberalism, but through terms that will be more sympathetic to object-oriented thought, which itself has been accused of neoliberal leanings.[44] Construing the subject as deconstructed, lateral, multiple, rhizomatic, etc., has yet to liberate subjects, but in fact has anticipated changes in the shape of forces of oppression, which in turn differently construe themselves against those same subjects of revision. Perhaps surprisingly, object-oriented theories may be able to accommodate Grosz's alternative. For example, we might locate a gesture toward imperceptibility in Graham Harman's withdrawn objects' reserve of inaccessible excess that prevents their being exhausted in and by networks of relations. Indeed, for Levi Bryant, withdrawal makes Harman's philosophy a "powerful challenge to . . . 'identity philosophy'" and "to the theory of calculation and mastery upon which neoliberal ideology is founded."[45] By veering away from identity and capture, withdrawn objects elicit the impersonal and imperceptible.

In her essay "The Impersonal Is Political: Spinoza and a Feminist Politics of Imperceptibility," Hasana Sharp further connects the impersonal forces of Grosz with Spinoza. To Sharp's thinking, Spinoza "offers [Grosz] a rubric of analysis that denies the radical uniqueness of human being with respect to the rest of nature."[46] Sharp writes, "A Spinozan politics necessarily entails the collaboration of others, but it is important to consider those others to include more than human beings, and to consider the causes and effects of our collective interaction in excess of consciousness or intersubjectivity."[47] Like Clough's conception of affect-itself in excess of body-as-organism, Spinoza's politics is grounded in matter or substance, and suggests radical continuity between all forms of being.[48]

Sharp associates Spinoza's "hyper-rational" political thought with Grosz's call for "greater abstraction in feminist theory."[49] Indeed, both thinkers arrive at inhumanism through abstraction, a process by which political existence shifts from being explicit to being vague. Abstraction creates big bodies through the move toward imperceptibility that Sharp identifies with Spinoza's "polemic" of "getting over oneself."[50]

While we may be tempted to understand imperceptibility as a "micro" relation, passing "below the radar" of perception, in this political dimension it is in fact best understood quite differently. Bigness does not make one more visible and specific; such bigness would only amount to being more vulnerable to capture and accountability. Counterintuitively, becoming big makes one more imperceptible and generic; this abstract bigness thwarts systems of control with illegibility. Hence, imperceptibility is not about disappearing into something "bigger than you," but about becoming indistinguishable from that bigness. When it comes to self and other kinds of information, the inclusive abstraction that dilates data makes these differences imperceptible. It is about being bigger than oneself, oneself: like Norman Bombardini, both self and aggregate.

Indeed, if bigness first swells a figure into oafish obviousness, the gross stereotype of individual obesity, abstraction quickly causes it to outgrow the figure's specificity. Becoming *even* bigger blurs the figure into a generic ground that forestalls conscious focus and recedes from perception. Like Bombardini eating on the edge of an abstraction in which the singular self gives way to populations and substance, here the gesture of inscribing a profile makes an abstract mark, "incorporating" diverse points into the same body. It is as much as to say, *these things are the same thing.*

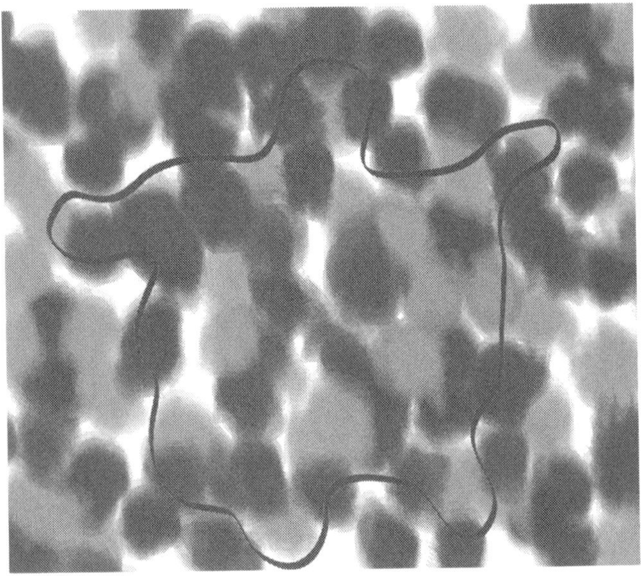

ONE

One persists

Bigness is sameness. It is thermodynamic entropy played out to the end. As Spinoza writes, "Nature is always the same."[51] With sameness, the imperceptibility advanced by a big body politics diverges from Grosz in a small but significant way. For Grosz, Nietzschean force is agonistic and fulfills itself in becoming.[52] Yet, this kind of dynamism feels alien to big being, which seems to need a decelerated form of force closer to mere, simple persistence. From point to line to plane to body, each aesthetic form we have considered has gradually expanded and gently decelerated expressions of self. So can we use this notion of deceleration to conceive a more lethargic politics?

For Spinoza, part of any being's essence is a power to act understood, as philosopher Steven Nadler explains, as a "power to persevere in being,"[53] which is to say, to hold an outline, to cohere in form, to persist. Much as Latour et al. advance persistence of form across gradual temporal change, Spinoza's term *conatus* describes this "kind of existential inertia."[54] Accordingly, political resistance in this model is not oppositional, not little, and not about action. For example, practices like sousveillance, in which small actors watch the big from below, are not what's at stake. Instead, a politics of imperceptibility mobilizes correspondences, vastness, and stasis.

In stasis, individual laborers cease to work and the commodity labor power ceases to function. Critics of object-oriented theory are mistaken to associate being an object with oppression. Not being an object, but being circulated as such in the generation of value, is what oppresses. And so deceleration grinds circulation to a near halt; bigness swallows value, the unevenness that is the motor of capitalism and exceptionalism; and labor power idles in a state of listlessness. When bigness can barely budge, exchangeability breaks down. The inertia of *conatus* sets in.

Here, a big body politics finds its ethics. Such slow bigness evokes the yogic principle of *ahimsa*, or nonviolence. In his commentary on "Book Two" of *The Yoga Sutras of Patanjali*, Sri Swami Satchidananda explains that ahimsa should not be understood as not acting violently, but as refraining from any harm, even so much as thinking harmful thoughts.[55] For Irina Aristarkhova, the practice of ahimsa in Jainism manifests the enlarged scope of transpecies feminist practices of care.[56] Care summons responsibility toward the otherwise-mattered populations and collective forms we have examined here.

Rubbing up close with otherness produces friction, like static electricity. Can we be static, nearly still? Bonded together in a static force field, difference generates dampened prickles of energy and even—persisting and tingling in stasis—awareness. Ahimsa stands aware as slow, considered mindfulness. This friction is no rapid, repellent antagonism—far from it. The extreme prudence in ahimsa requires a radical slowdown to a pace against which the momentum of reactivity no longer holds sway.

Ahimsa is an aspect of the first of the eight limbs of yoga, *yama*, which Satchidananda translates as "abstinence." Yama is the abstention from the very assertion of self, like Berlant's self-abeyance. Rather than acting with force or reacting to force, yama abstains from any agitations. So, too, the politics of decelerationist aesthetics slumps against connections and correlations, along with the politics of recognition and even representation. In such a spirit, François Laruelle's One summons radical inclusiveness in the manifold-turned-singular, evoking the "more" we associate with bigness (and the geometrical structure adopted here):

> The One is immanence (to) itself
> without constituting a point, a plane,
> without withdrawing or folding
> back upon itself. It is One-in-One,
> that which can only be found in the
> One, not with Being or the Other. It
> is a radical rather than an absolute
> immanence. The 'more' immanence
> is radical, the 'more' it is universal or
> gives-in-immanence philosophy itself
> (the World, etc.).[57]

In his hyperobjects, Timothy Morton bounces object-oriented thinking up a level to the vastness of ecological scale and geological time. Like geologic sediment, a big body politics is unconcerned with minutia like mere human life, and the other bits, informational and otherwise, that compose it. Lethargically, separation converges in One. Things settle, and entropy overrides variation. Sharp apprises us that "[a] feminist politics of imperceptibility simply siphons enabling energy and power wherever it happens to find it."[58] Drawing a line through geologic time, a "slow death" of populations eases in, coming to embody a subtle standstill. "Inside this circle," Latour et al. explain, "everything might change through time. . . . What matters is that the change be gradual enough to preserve some continuity."[59]

Imperceptibly, all things persist, existing as a way of insisting, silently stating for the record that big being *is*.

Notes

1 Object-oriented feminism (OOF) is a new field of analysis, which has been developing through panels I organized at the Society for Literature, Science, and the Arts from 2010 to 2015, and dialogues around a forthcoming volume, Katherine Behar, ed., *Object-Oriented Feminism* (Minneapolis: University of Minnesota Press, 2016).

2 The term *accelerationism*, first coined by Benjamin Noys, was adopted by Nick Srnicek and Alex Williams in their "Accelerationist Manifesto." For an anthology of accelerationist thought, including Srnicek and Williams's manifesto, see Robin Mackay and Armen Avanessian, eds., *#Accelerate: The Accelerationist Reader* (Falmouth, UK: Urbanomic, 2014). On aesthetics and accelerationism, see Steven Shaviro, *No Speed Limit: Three Essays on Accelerationism* (Minneapolis: University of Minnesota Press, 2015); see also Gean Moreno, "Editorial—'Accelerationist Aesthetics,'"

e-flux journal, no. 46 (June 2013), accessed February 9, 2016, http://www.e-flux.com/issues/46-june-2013/.

3 Quoted in Colin Brown, "The Rise and Rise of Datanomics," *CNBC Business*, June 2011, accessed August 12, 2012, http://www.cnbcmagazine.com/story/the-rise-and-rise-of-datanomics/1394/1/.

4 This practice is not unique to digital data. For an account of postwar analog profiling, see Sarah E. Igo, *The Averaged American: Surveys, Citizens, and the Making of a Mass Public* (Cambridge: Harvard University Press, 2007).

5 The White House, "Consumer Data Privacy in a Networked World: A Framework for Protecting Privacy and Promoting Innovation in the Global Digital Economy," February 23, 2012, accessed August 12, 2012, http://www.whitehouse.gov/sites/default/files/privacy-final.pdf.

6 Many examples can be found online, for example, Do Not Track, accessed August 12, 2012, http://donottrack.us/; TrackMeNot, accessed August 12, 2012, http://trackmenot.org.

7 For example, see Omer Tene and Jules Polonetsky, "Privacy in the Age of Big Data: A Time for Big Decisions," *Stanford Law Review Online* 64 (February 2, 2012): 63–69, accessed August 12, 2012, http://www.stanfordlawreview.org/online/privacy-paradox/big-data; Molly Wood, "In the world of Big Data, privacy invasion is the business model," *CBS News Tech T@lk*, accessed August 12, 2012, http://

www.cbsnews.com/8301-501465_162-57388439-501465/in-the-world-of-big-data-privacy-invasion-is-the-business-model/; Howard Wen, "Big ethics for big data: How businesses can confront the ethical issues tied to massive aggregation and data analysis," *O'Reilly Radar*, June 11, 2012, accessed August 12, 2012, http://radar.oreilly.com/2012/06/ethics-big-data-business-decisions.html.

8 David Harvey, "The Body as Accumulation Strategy," in *Spaces of Hope* (Los Angeles: University of California Press, 2000), 107.

9 Ibid.

10 The White House, "Consumer Data Privacy."

11 See United States Department of Labor, "Occupational Safety and Health Administration," accessed August 12, 2012, http://www.osha.gov/.

12 Again, examples proliferate. See "The Data Deluge," *Economist*, February 25, 2010, accessed July 14, 2012, http://www.economist.com/node/15579717; Dan Roffman, "Data Deluge: The Problem Is, You Can't Keep Everything," *Forbes*, July 5, 2012, accessed July 14, 2012, http://www.forbes.com/sites/ciocentral/2012/07/05/data-deluge-the-problem-is-you-cant-keep-everything/; Nick Bilton, "At Davos: Discussion of a Global Data Deluge," *New York Times*, January 25, 2012, accessed July 14, 2012, http://bits.blogs.nytimes.com/2012/01/25/at-davos-discussions-of-a-global-data-deluge/.

13 Colin Brown, "The Rise and Rise."

14 Bruno Latour et al., "'The whole is always smaller than its parts'—a digital test of Gabriel Tarde's monads," *British Journal of Sociology* 63, no. 4 (December 2012): 606.

15 Ibid., 598.

16 Bogost borrows *ontography* from Graham Harman, who discovered the term in a short story, "Oh Whistle and I'll Come to You, My Lad," by M. R. James. See Graham Harman, "ontography: the rise of objects," July 14, 2009, accessed September 15, 2012, http://doctorzamalek2.wordpress.com/2009/07/14/ontography-the-rise-of-objects/; see also Ian Bogost, *Alien Phenomenology, Or, What It's Like to Be a Thing* (Minneapolis: University of Minnesota Press, 2012), 38.

17 Bogost, *Alien Phenomenology.*

18 Ibid., 40.

19 Ibid., 38.

20 Latour et al., "The Whole," 607.

21 Bogost, *Alien Phenomenology,* 58.

22 David Berry, "The Uses of Object-Oriented Ontology," *Stunlaw: A critical review of politics, arts and technology,* May 25, 2012, accessed August 1, 2015, http://stunlaw.blogspot.nl/2012/05/uses-of-object-oriented-ontology.html.

23 Latour et al., "The Whole," 599.

24 David Foster Wallace, *The Broom of the System* (New York: Avon Books, 1987), 96–105.

25 Lauren Berlant, "Slow Death (Sovereignty, Obesity,

Lateral Agency)," *Critical Inquiry* 33 (Summer 2007): 754–80.

26 Ibid.," 771–72.

27 Ibid.," 757.

28 Ibid.

29 Ibid., 763.

30 Bogost, *Alien Phenomenology*, 59.

31 Berlant, "Slow Death," 779.

32 Ibid.

33 Ibid., 763.

34 Patricia Ticineto Clough et al., "Notes Towards a Theory of Affect-Itself," *ephemera* 7, no. 1 (February 2007): 60–77.

35 Ibid., 62–63.

36 Ibid., 64.

37 Ibid., 62.

38 Ibid., 65.

39 Berlant, "Slow Death," 778.

40 Elizabeth Grosz, "A politics of imperceptibility: A response to 'Anti-racism, multiculturalism and the ethics of identification,'" *Philosophy & Social Criticism* 28, no. 4 (2002): 465.

41 Ibid., 467.

42 Hasana Sharp, "The Impersonal Is Political: Spinoza and a Feminist Politics of Imperceptibility," *Hypatia* 24, no. 4 (Fall 2009): 84–103.

43 Quoted in ibid., 94.

44 See Alexander R. Galloway, "The Poverty of Philosophy: Realism and Post-Fordism," *Critical*

Inquiry 39, no. 2 (Winter 2013): 347–66; and Alexander R. Galloway, "A response to Graham Harman's 'Marginalia on Radical Thinking,'" June 3, 2012, accessed July 14, 2012, http://itself.wordpress.com/2012/06/03/a-response-to-graham-harmans-marginalia-on-radical-thinking/.

45 Levi Bryant, "Harman, Withdrawal, and Vacuum Packed Objects: My Gratitude," May 30, 2012, accessed September 15, 2012, http://larvalsubjects.wordpress.com/2012/05/30/harman-withdrawal-and-vacuum-packed-objects-my-gratitude/.

46 Sharp, "The Impersonal is Political," 92.

47 Ibid., 95.

48 For example, Spinoza's theory of "adequate knowledge" uses the radical, homogeneous continuity of substance as a way out of Cartesian correlationism (which makes this thinking especially suitable for an object-oriented feminist project). For Spinoza, mind and body are two expressions of the same substance. This continuity provides the "adequate knowledge" to know God.

49 Sharp, "The Impersonal is Political," 97.

50 Ibid., 94.

51 Steven Nadler, "Baruch Spinoza," in *The Stanford Encyclopedia of Philosophy*, ed. Edward N. Zalta, spring 2011 ed., accessed July 14, 2012, http://plato.stanford.edu/entries/spinoza/#PasAct.

52 Grosz, "A politics of imperceptibility," 466.

53 Nadler, "Baruch Spinoza."

54 Ibid.

55 *The Yoga Sutras of Patanjali*, trans. and commentary by Sri Swami Satchidananda (Yogaville: Integral Yoga Publications, 2011), 125–26.

56 Irina Aristarkhova, "Thou Shall Not Harm All Living Beings: Feminism, Jainism, and Animals," *Hypatia* 27, no. 3 (Summer 2012): 636–50.

57 François Laruelle, "A Summary of Non-Philosophy," *Pli* 8 (1999): 141.

58 Sharp, "The Impersonal is Political," 101.

59 Latour et al., "The Whole," 610.

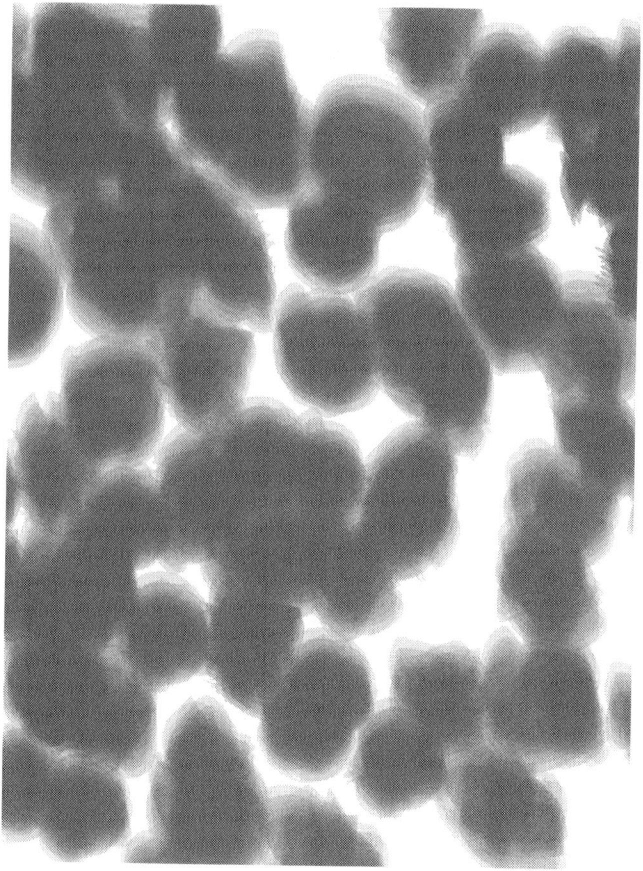

Interdisciplinary artist Katherine Behar is assistant professor of New Media Arts at Baruch College, City University of New York. She is the editor of *Object-Oriented Feminism*, forthcoming from University of Minnesota Press, and the coauthor, with Emmy Mikelson, of *And Another Thing: Nonanthropocentrism and Art.*

Made in United States
Orlando, FL
04 November 2026

90204442R00042